DESIGN A PRAM

ANNE FINE

Illustrated by
PHILIPPE DUPASQUIER

0064375902

William Heinemann Ltd
Michelin House
81 Fulham Road
London SW3 6RB

LONDON   MELBOURNE   AUCKLAND

First published in 1991
Text © Anne Fine 1991
Illustrations © Philippe Dupasquier 1991
ISBN 0 434 97672 5

Printed in Italy
by Olivotto

A school pack of BANANA BOOKS 43-48 is
available from Heinemann Educational Books
ISBN 0 435 00107 8

Thinking of Something For Them to Do

MR OAKWAY LOOKED at them with his hunted look.

'You've all drawn a map of your desks,' he said.

'Yes,' they all yelled.

'And you've all drawn a map of the classroom.'

'Yes,' they all yelled.

'And you've all drawn a map of the school and the playground and the staff car park.'

'Yes,' they all yelled.

'Right, then,' he said. 'Design a pram.'

They all looked at one another and made funny faces. Design a pram? Why? How?

'Why?' asked Hetty. 'Why do you want us to design a pram?'

'How?' Oliver demanded. 'How?'

Mr Oakway didn't answer. He was standing on tiptoe in front of the cupboard, rooting through all the stuff at the back of one of the shelves.

'Report cards . . .' he muttered. 'Where are they? Where did I put them?'

Report cards! Everyone stared at the calendar on the wall. End of term in ten days . . .

'Right,' said Hetty. 'We're all going to design a pram. We'll split ourselves up into two teams. Then we'll have a competition. Each team gets to design their own pram secretly in their own corner. They'll draw it and describe it on a huge sheet of paper. And Mr Oakway gets to be the judge.'

There were murmurs from the back of the classroom.

'Oh, no! Not Mr Oakway judging!'

'He never *chooses*.'

'He never picks a real winner.'

Hetty ignored the murmurings. She turned to Mr Oakway who was tugging a box of report cards out of the cupboard, spilling everything all over himself and the floor.

'Is that all right?' she asked.

'What?' said Mr Oakway. 'Is what all right?'

'Hetty's bossing everyone about again,' explained Oliver. 'She's making it into a competition and she's dividing us up into two teams. Each team designs a pram secretly in their own corner on a big sheet of paper, and you get to be the judge.'

Mr Oakway looked up from his clutter of spilt report cards.

'Secretly?' he said. 'Do you mean that you'll all be whispering quietly in corners?'

He stood up. Peeling a golden star off the sheet lying on his desk, he came across the classroom and stuck it firmly on Hetty's forehead.

'She is bossy,' he admitted to the rest of them. 'But I couldn't manage without her. She runs this classroom brilliantly. And today she's in charge.'

And, since he was about to write their report cards, for once nobody in the class even thought of arguing.

Picking the Two Team Leaders

'RIGHT,' SAID HETTY. 'I'll tell you how we're going to divide up into teams. We're going to do it by picksies.'

'Who's going to pick?'

'We'll vote,' said Hetty. 'Everyone gets to vote for two pickers, and the pickers get to pick the teams. So the first thing everyone needs is two little squares of paper and a pencil.'

Chad went up to Mr Oakway's desk and took a few sheets out of the paper tray. He tore them into little squares, and handed everyone two.

'No talking,' said Hetty. 'No discussing and no favours, and no just picking your best friend. You have to vote for whoever it is you really think will be the best team leader to design a pram.'

Everyone sat quietly, sucking their pencils and having a think. From time to time their eyes rested on another person and gradually, one by one, each of them took their pencils out of their mouths and wrote down a name on one piece of paper.

And then another name on the other piece of paper.

'Can we vote for the same person twice?' asked Sareena.

'Certainly not,' said Hetty.

'Why not?' asked Oliver Smart. 'There's no reason why we shouldn't. If you really, really want a particular person to be a team leader, you should be able to give them both your votes. Why on earth not?'

'Because I say so,' said Hetty. And that was that, because Mr Oakway had announced that although Hetty was bossy, she ran the classroom brilliantly, and today she was in charge. And he *was* writing their report cards . . .

So everyone, even Oliver Smart, meekly wrote down two separate names on the two little squares of paper. And Chad went round the class collecting them up. Oliver and Sareena turned their backs on the class and dealt them into little piles, and counted them. Then Oliver turned round.

'As the returning officer for this classroom,' he announced. 'I declare that the two team leaders for the Great Design a Pram Competition are –'

He kept them all waiting just long enough to annoy them.

'Myself (Oliver Smart) and Hetty Maloney!'

There were murmurs from the back of the classroom.

'Of course – the Two Bossies!'

'Typical!'

And, more sarcastically:

'Well, what a surprise!'

'Fancy that!'

Picking the Two Teams

'MOIRA,' SAID HETTY.

'Wayne,' said Oliver.

'Suzie,' said Hetty.

'Douglas,' said Oliver.

'Lorraine,' said Hetty.

'Sareena,' said Oliver.

'I wanted Sareena,' said Hetty. 'I was going to ask for Sareena next. I'll tell you what, I'll swap you Sareena for two goes in a row.'

'I don't want two goes in a row,' said Oliver. 'I want Sareena. That's why I picked her.'

'Listen,' said Hetty. 'I'm making you a perfectly reasonable offer. Two people in a row for Sareena.'

'No,' said Oliver. 'Sareena is in my team.'

'No, she isn't,' said Hetty. 'She's in my team. I want her and I'm going to have her. Come over here, Sareena.'

Sareena looked anxious. First she looked anxiously at Oliver and his team,

then she looked anxiously at Hetty, and hers. Then she shrugged and walked over to join the people in Hetty's team.

'Hetty, you are so bossy!' said Oliver. But he didn't dare complain to Mr Oakway because he was sitting at his desk, writing their reports.

'Your turn to pick,' said Hetty. 'Hurry up and get on with it.'

So Oliver got on with it. He picked Ahmed and Laura and Roy and Jamie D. and Philip and Chad and Stephen, while

Hetty chose Elinor and Jamie B. and Anna
and Neeta and Tracey.

'That's it, then,' announced Hetty,
looking around at her team. 'Even-
stevens. And if Vicky gets back from the
dentist, I get her.'

Some of the muttering started up again
at the back.

' . . . so *bossy* . . .'

' . . . thinks she runs the whole
world . . .'

'. . . hope he finishes those reports
soon. Can't stand much more of
this . . . '

But nobody complained very loudly, in
case it was their report Mr Oakway was in
the middle of writing.

Suzie Changes Sides

'RIGHT,' SAID HETTY to the members of her team. 'We shall work in whispers. No one must say anything louder than a whisper. If you talk loudly, Oliver Smart's lot will hear, and they'll pinch all our bright ideas.'

'What bright ideas?' asked Jamie B.

Hetty gave Jamie B. a bit of the old evil eye before turning her attention back to the others.

'Moira,' she said. 'You're the best drawer in our team so you can do the picture and Lorraine can do the labels.'

'What labels?'

'The labels for our pram design, explaining what all the bits are and how they work. We're going to design a pram

that a baby would be proud to sit in. It will be beautiful and comfy and interesting and educational. It'll be the best pram in the world. It'll be so good, the baby won't ever want to get out of it.'

'Then it should have a waterbed mattress,' said Elinor. 'My uncle's girlfriend has a waterbed and it's brilliant. It's like lolling about on a cloud.'

'Right, then,' agreed Hetty. 'A waterbed mattress.'

'The pram should have a mobile circling overhead,' said Tracey. 'In case the baby wants something to watch. Silver dolphins. Golden swallows.'

'Music!' cried Neeta, clapping her hands. 'As the wheels go round, they should wind up a musical box that plays sweet tunes whenever the pram stops.'

'We should have a motor for the wheels,' said Suzie. 'So no one has to push. And maybe we should have knives sticking out of the wheel rims to keep fierce dogs away.'

The rest of the team turned to stare at her.

'Knives? Sticking out of the *wheels*?'

'That's disgusting!'

'And it's dangerous.'

'You could cut a puppy to ribbons if you had sharp blades sticking out of the wheels!'

'We're not having that, are we, Hetty?'

Voices were getting raised. They weren't working in whispers any longer.

'Ssssh!' Hetty ordered. 'The others will hear. They'll pinch our ideas.'

'They're welcome to that idea,' said Elinor. 'They can have it. It's disgusting.'

And she glowered at Suzie.

Suzie flushed scarlet.

'If my idea is so disgusting,' she said, 'maybe I shouldn't be in your team at all. Maybe I should be in the other team!'

Hetty faced her out.

'Maybe you should,' she said.

'All right, then,' said Suzie, very hurt indeed. 'If that's how you feel'

And, without another word, she gathered up her things and stalked across the room to join Oliver Smart's team.

Some of the people in Hetty's team wanted to call her back, but Hetty wouldn't let them. They didn't argue for long. After all, Mr Oakway had told them she ran the classroom brilliantly, and she was in charge. And he *was* busy writing their reports . . .

Even-stevens

IN OLIVER SMART'S team, there was a whisper argument raging about how the pram should be steered.

'Remote control,' insisted Douglas. 'What we need is a really good computer that stays in the house. Then whoever is controlling the pram just sits at home pressing the right buttons, or using a joystick, and the pram goes forwards or backwards, left or right.'

'We'll need a camera on the front of the pram, then. It sends live film of where the pram's going back to Mission Control.'

'The pram should be rocket-propelled,' said Ahmed. 'For fast speeds. And it should have retros for instant braking.'

'In that case we'll need it to be a lot more

streamline than the one Philip's
drawing,' said Stephen. 'Rub out the
front, Philip, and draw it again, much
more pointy.'

'What about the baby?' asked Roy.

'The baby will just have to be squashed up at the back,' said Laura. 'It's a bit safer up at the back, anyway, at high speeds.'

'We could give the baby a gamma ray gun,' suggested Douglas. 'Then it could pick off anyone who was sneaking up behind it.'

'Not "it",' said Jamie D. 'Babies aren't "it"!' He wasn't whispering any longer. He was talking quite loudly. 'Babies are "he" or "she". Little boys or little girls. And they're far too young to be out on their own in a remote-controlled pram. Babies need looking after all the time. In fact they're happiest when they can hear a recording of their own mother's heartbeat close to them. They certainly shouldn't be encouraged to sit up and shoot people out of their prams.'

He looked up. Everyone else in the
team was scowling at him, so he looked
down again quickly.

'They wouldn't need to sit up and
shoot people,' said Suzie, 'if you had
sharp knives sticking out of the wheels.'

'Knives sticking out of the wheels!
Brilliant!'

'That's a really good idea! You're a
genius, Suzie! Do you want to join our
team?'

'Yes, please,' said Suzie. 'I wasn't
getting on too well over with that lot.'

Oliver Smart looked anxious.

'If you join us,' he said. 'It won't be fair. We'll have more people in our team than they have in theirs.'

'We could send someone over to them . . . '

Everyone turned to look at Jamie D., who flushed a deep scarlet.

'I see,' he said at last. 'Well, if that's how you all feel, I think perhaps I will go over and join Hetty's team.'

'You'll get on better there, I expect,' said Suzie. 'There are quite a lot of softies already in that team. All on about fluffy cushions and tinkling music and furry pram linings.'

The rest of Oliver Smart's team burst out into sniggers.

'Tinkling music!'

'Fluffy cushions!'

'Furry pram linings!'

Silently, Jamie D. gathered up his belongings and made his way over the classroom to Hetty's group, busily whispering in the corner.

Judging the Competition

MR OAKWAY SAT at his desk for a whole hour, busily writing reports. Meanwhile the members of Oliver Smart's team improved the design of their pram by adding bright flashing lights to warn pedestrians of its approach, a siren to alert road traffic, a handle the baby could pull to release a cloud of poisonous black smoke behind the pram as it raced along the streets, and a bullet-proof hood, just in case.

At the same time, the members of Hetty Maloney's team added safety parking lights, a little firework display attachment to keep the baby amused on dark evenings, soft woolly fingers that popped out of the sides of the pram to stroke the baby whenever the mother's heartbeat tape was playing, and a better way of braking on steep hills, just in case.

Then they quietly drew their chairs up around the large piece of paper on which Moira had so carefully drawn the design of their pram. Lorraine wrote nice neat labels, and they coloured little patterns all around the edges.

Oliver Smart's team looked across, guessed what they were doing, drew their chairs round their sheet of paper, and copied them. Nobody dared complain, because Mr Oakway was doing the reports.

Then Mr Oakway finished. He could hardly believe it. He was just stuffing the last report into its little brown envelope when Hetty fixed him with a beady eye.

'Time to judge,' she told him firmly.

Mr Oakway pushed his chair back and strolled across to look at the designs. He admired pretty well everything on each of them, down to the patterns round the edges. But he particularly seemed to admire Suzie's knives revolving on the wheels to keep any fierce dogs away, and Jamie D.'s soothing tape of the heartbeat.

'It's so hard to judge,' he complained. 'I mean, here's one pram: a magnificent machine – goes like the wind, tough as a tank, and any baby would feel safe surrounded by wild animals and drunk drivers and even armed bank robbers.'

Shaking his head in wonder, he turned to the other sheet of paper.

'But then, here's the other: luxurious beyond any baby's dreams – safe, warm, and chockful of comforts and pleasures!'

He turned to face them. They knew exactly what was coming.

'I can't decide,' he said. 'You can't compare two prams as different as this. Each in its own way is a masterpiece of design. They're both quite wonderful. So I'm afraid they'll *both* have to win.'

Oh, he was hopeless! Every time! What was the *point* of having competitions if the judge was too soft to pick a real winner?

There was quite a bit of muttering from the back of the class.

' . . . every single *time* . . . '

' . . . doesn't even *try* . . . '

' . . . absolutely *pathetic* . . . '

Everyone turned to Hetty.

Hetty sighed. She glanced down at the two huge sheets of paper: her team's floating bubble of heavenly delights, and the other team's great travelling fortress of power.

'He's right,' she told the class. 'He isn't usually, when he can't choose. But this time he is right. They're both so different and they're both so good, that they should both win. We'll have to let him off.'

There were a few discontented murmurs, but, on the whole, everyone took it rather well, considering.

Relieved, Mr Oakway picked off a second gold star and stuck it on Hetty's forehead.

'You are a gem,' he said. 'You know I couldn't run this class without you. Will you look after them while I nip along the corridor and through to the office with these reports?'

'All right,' said Hetty. 'But don't be too long.'

'I won't,' he said. 'I'll be two minutes. You'll think of something to do, won't you?'

'Oh yes,' said Hetty. 'I'll think of something.'

And she did. Before he was even out of the door, she was standing on her chair, holding an auction.

'What am I bid for these two beautiful golden stars?' she cried. 'A comic? An apple? First go at skipping? What am I bid?'